THE SHAPING AND RESHAPING OF EARTH'S SURFACE™

Metamorphic Rocks
and the Rock Cycle

Joanne Mattern

The Rosen Publishing Group's

PowerKids Press™

New York

Published in 2006 by The Rosen Publishing Group, Inc.
29 East 21st Street, New York, NY 10010

First Edition

Editor: Melissa Acevedo
Book Design: Ginny Chu

Photo Credits: Cover, pp. 1, 4 (bottom) © Steve Austin; Papilio/Corbis; p. 4 (top) © Tom Bean/Corbis; p. 4 (top) © Gary Braasch/Corbis; pp. 6, 7 Ginny Chu/Rosen Publishing; p. 8 © Royalty-Free/Corbis; p. 8 (left) © Steve Kaufman/Corbis; p. 10 © Jim Sugar/Corbis; pp. 12, 13 USGS / This Dynamic Earth; p. 13 (right) © Lloyd Cluff/Corbis; p. 14 © Hubert Stadler/Corbis; p. 14 (top left) © M. Angelo/Corbis; p. 14 (top right) © Neil Rabinowitz/Corbis; p. 16 (top left) © Fritz Polking; Frank Lane Picture Agency/Corbis; p. 16 (bottom left) © Charles Mauzy/Corbis; p. 16 (right) © Richard Hamilton Smith/Corbis; p. 18 © Nathan Benn/Corbis; p. 20 Kurt Hollocher, Union College Geology Department.

Library of Congress Cataloging-in-Publication Data

Mattern, Joanne, 1963–
Metamorphic rocks and the rock cycle / Joanne Mattern.
p. cm. — (The shaping and reshaping of earth's surface) Includes bibliographical references and index. ISBN 1-4042-3194-3 (lib. bdg.)
1. Rocks, Metamorphic—Juvenile literature. 2. Geochemical cycles—Juvenile literature. I. Title. II. Series.
QE475.A2M395 2006
552'.4—dc22

2004023029

Manufactured in the United States of America

Contents

Serpentinite is a metamorphic rock that can be scratched easily with a knife.

Found along the Illinois River in Oregon, this schist rock has lines of quartz.

The word "metamorphic" refers to something that changes. Metamorphic rocks got their name because they are formed when one kind of rock changes into a different kind of rock.

Right:
This is a close-up view of a cliff made of granite gneiss rock.

Metamorphic Rocks

What Is Metamorphic Rock?

Earth is made up of three kinds of rock, called igneous, sedimentary, and metamorphic. Like our planet, these rocks are always changing. Igneous and sedimentary rocks can change because of strong heat or pressure. A new kind of rock is formed from this change. New rock that is formed from heat or pressure is called metamorphic rock.

Metamorphic rocks have been on Earth for millions of years. They can be different shapes, sizes, and colors. Metamorphic rocks are used to make buildings, jewelry, powders, and other things. They are an important part of our world.

Metamorphic rocks have been on Earth for millions of years. They can be different shapes, sizes, and colors.

Metamorphic Rocks in the Rock Cycle

The rocks that make up our planet are constantly changing through a process called the rock cycle. In this process old rocks are broken down to form new ones. Through the rock cycle, the several layers that make up Earth are always changing, too. Earth's top layer is called the crust. It is made of rock. Below the crust is a layer of hot liquid called magma. Earth's core is the next layer. The core has two layers. The outer layer is made of melted metals. The inner layer is a solid ball of metal.

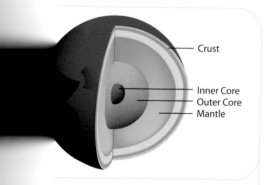

Crust

Inner Core
Outer Core
Mantle

The above picture shows the different layers of Earth.

The rock cycle starts when hot magma flows through cracks in Earth's crust. Once on the surface, the magma cools and hardens into igneous rocks. When these igneous rocks wear down, they settle to the bottoms of rivers and oceans. Over time they form layers of sediment. Pressure changes these layers into

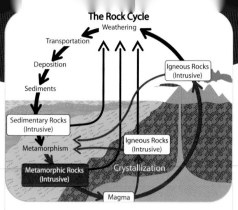

The Rock Cycle

This diagram shows the changing of old rocks into new ones through the rock cycle. Metamorphic rocks form through strong heat and pressure.

sedimentary rocks. Strong heat and pressure can cause these rocks to change from an igneous or sedimentary rock into a metamorphic rock. Metamorphic rocks then break down over time and form new layers of sediment. This forms sedimentary rocks. The rock cycle continues!

The rocks that make up our planet are constantly changing through a process called the rock cycle.

This picture shows the metamorphic rock quartzite in Israel.

What do the Rocky Mountains, the Alps, and the Himalayas all have in common? They are made mostly of metamorphic rocks!

Right:
The metamorphic rock quartzite is one of the major rocks that make up the Rocky Mountains in Colorado.

How Metamorphic Rocks Are Formed

Under Pressure

Metamorphic rocks can form in two different ways. One way is through major pressure inside Earth. Earth's layers are heavy and they press down on each other. This causes pressure to build up. The pressure pushes or forces rocks into one another. The rocks are put under so much pressure that it causes their minerals to change. This creates metamorphic rocks.

When this strong pressure continues, sometimes the metamorphic rocks are pushed up and out of the crust. This creates mountains. Most of Earth's mountains are made of metamorphic rocks.

Earth's layers are heavy and they press down on each other. This causes pressure to build up.

The Heat Is On

Forces inside Earth do not just create pressure. They also create heat. When Earth's layers are pressing down on each other and creating pressure, they force hot magma up toward the surface. Sometimes this magma escapes through volcanoes when they erupt. Other times just a small amount of magma is able to push through a crack in Earth's crust. This is called

This picture shows the Kilauea Volcano in Hawaii. It erupted in 1984.

a magma surge.

A volcanic eruption or a magma surge creates a large amount of heat on Earth's surface, making the rocks around the magma very hot. The rocks can become so hot that the minerals inside the rock change. The minerals can change so much that they form a new kind of rock, a metamorphic rock. Metamorphic rocks form when the temperature around rocks gets as hot as 300 to 2,000° F (149 to 1,093° C).

Can lightning form a rock?

The answer is yes! When lightning strikes sand, it can change the sand into a metamorphic rock called fulgurite.

Metamorphic rocks form when the temperature around rocks gets as hot as 300 to 2,000° F (150 to 1,000° C).

Plates on the Move

Earth's crust is not one solid piece. It is made of large pieces called plates. These plates move around on top of the layer of liquid magma. This means that Earth's surface is always moving.

Even though we cannot feel Earth's surface move, metamorphic rocks are proof of Earth's movement. Sometimes the plates bump into each other. This can push the land up to create mountains. The pressure that forces these rocks out also changes their minerals. This is why mountains are mostly made up of metamorphic rocks.

Sometimes plates scrape against each other. This forms a weak spot in the crust called a

The above picture shows some of the large pieces, called plates, that make up the crust of our planet. Each plate has been named by scientists who studied their movements.

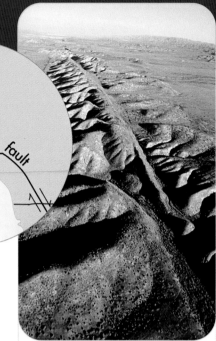

fault line. When the pressure inside Earth gets too strong, the plates shift so much that an earthquake occurs along the fault line. Volcanoes can also form along fault lines. Hot magma can burst through these cracks and reach the surface. The tremendous heat and pressure of volcanoes and earthquakes change the molecules in the rocks, creating metamorphic rocks.

The San Andreas Fault in California is known for its many earthquakes.

Sometimes plates scrape against each other. This forms a weak spot in the crust called a fault line.

13

Slate is a type of foliated rock. You can tell it is foliated by the cracks.

Marble is a nonfoliated metamorphic rock. It is used for building.

Scientists study what metamorphic rocks are made of by breaking them into small pieces. Then they cut a thin piece of the rock and look at it under a microscope. This allows the scientists to see the minerals inside the rock. Scientists also break the rock into powder to study the minerals inside.

Right:
These red granite rocks can be found along the water in Brittany, France.

Kinds of Metamorphic Rocks

Foliated and Nonfoliated

Sometimes pressure forces the minerals in metamorphic rocks into wavy lines. This creates a foliated rock. Slate is a kind of foliated rock.

Other metamorphic rocks are nonfoliated. These rocks are smoother and often form from heat or low pressure over a long period of time. Hornfels is an example of a nonfoliated rock.

Scientists can tell what a metamorphic rock used to be by studying the minerals inside it. The nonfoliated metamorphic rock marble is formed from limestone, a sedimentary rock. Scientists are able to see the mineral calcite in marble.

Scientists can tell what a metamorphic rock used to be by studying the minerals inside it.

Gneiss, Slate, and Schist

This picture of a gneiss rock was taken at Bayerischer Wald National Park in Germany. Gneiss is known as one of the toughest rocks in the world.

Gneiss is one of the most well known metamorphic rocks. It is formed when heat or pressure changes an igneous rock called granite. Gneiss is foliated and has many stripes in it. These stripes are formed because the minerals in the rock separate into layers as the metamorphic rock is formed.

A sedimentary rock called shale can change into a metamorphic rock called slate. Shale is formed from sediment in rivers and lakes, which has been

Slate is used to make tiles on the roofs of houses and to create sidewalks.

Schist contains a mineral called mica, which makes it flaky and hard to use.

pressed together over time to form a rock. Shale becomes slate through low heat or pressure. Slate is hard and breaks easily into flat pieces. It is usually gray, but it can also be red, black, green, or purple.

Garnets are often used to make jewelry. They are the birthstone for people who are born in the month of January.

Slate also changes into a different kind of metamorphic rock called schist. Schist forms when slate reaches a high temperature. Schists are valuable because the minerals in them often form a gem called garnet. Garnets are usually red, but they can also be yellow, light green, or even colorless.

A sedimentary rock called shale can change into a metamorphic rock called slate.

Marble, Quartzite, and Hornfels

One well-known metamorphic rock is marble. Formed from the sedimentary rock limestone, marble is made mostly of the mineral calcite. Pure marble is soft and can be scratched with a knife. It is often white but can be yellowish brown, black, red, or green. Different colors are the result of faults in the limestone from which the marble formed. Marble is the most widely used metamorphic rock because it is easily carved into statues and stones used for building.

Quartzite is an important metamorphic rock. It is a very hard rock that can scratch glass and is sometimes used to build roads. It forms when sandstone, a

...is statue in Glasgow, ...otland, is made from ...e nonfoliated ...etamorphic rock ...arble. The statue is ...cated in Glasgow's ...oyal Botanic Garden.

sedimentary rock, is changed by heat and pressure inside Earth. Quartzite is one of the major rocks that formed the Rocky Mountains.

Diamonds are sometimes found in metamorphic rocks. They are the hardest naturally occurring element in the world. They are also one of the most valuable. Diamond jewelry is very expensive. Diamonds are usually clear but can come in any color.

Another type of metamorphic rock is hornfels. This rock forms when a sedimentary rock called shale comes in contact with hot magma at temperatures from 392 to 1,472° F (200 to 800° C). Hornfels is a hard rock that comes in dark colors, either grey or black. It is used to create roads.

Pure marble is soft and can be scratched with a knife. It is white but can be yellowish brown, black, red, or green.

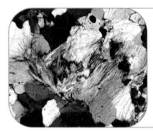

Sillimanite, a metamorphic rock mineral, is used to make car parts.

Andalusite is a metamorphic rock mineral. It is used as a gemstone.

Quartz is a hard mineral that is often used to make jewelry. It is found in metamorphic rocks and in igneous and sedimentary rocks, too.

Right:
Kyanite, another metamorphic rock mineral, forms in low temperatures.

Minerals in Metamorphic Rocks

Useful Minerals

Metamorphic rocks often contain minerals not found in other rocks. This is because the minerals were changed by the strong heat and pressure that created the rocks. The changed minerals include kyanite, sillimanite, and andalusite. These minerals can withstand very high temperatures and are strong. They are often used to make insulation for heating and electrical machinery.

The minerals in a metamorphic rock help scientists identify the rock. A metamorphic rock called chromite contains a mineral called chromium.

A metamorphic rock called chromite contains a mineral called chromium.

The Importance of Metamorphic Rocks

Metamorphic rocks are very useful. People use them to make different things. Buildings, roads, jewelry, and insulation are a few of the things made from metamorphic rocks and their minerals.

Metamorphic rocks are also an important part of Earth. These rocks help scientists learn about Earth's plates and their movements. The rocks' appearance, location, and minerals provide clues and facts about changes above and below Earth's surface.

The rock cycle has been changing Earth for millions of years. Metamorphic rocks are an important part of that change. They are part of the process that creates new rocks. The rock cycle will continue as long as Earth does. Metamorphic rocks will help that cycle go on.

Glossary

core (KOR) The hot center of Earth that is made of liquid rock.

crust (KRUST) The outer, or top, layer of a planet.

fault line (FAWLT LYN) The place on Earth's surface where two plates meet.

foliated (FOH-lee-ayt-ed) Having to do with metamorphic rocks that have minerals in wavy lines or bands.

igneous (IG-nee-us) Having to do with a hot, liquid, underground mineral that has cooled and hardened.

insulation (in-suh-LAY-shun) Matter that does not conduct heat or electricity.

jewelry (JOO-ul-ree) Objects worn for decoration that are made of special metals, such as gold and silver, and prized stones.

magma (MAG-muh) Hot, liquid rock beneath Earth's surface.

metamorphic (meh-tuh-MOR-fik) Having to do with rock that has been changed by heat and heavy weight.

minerals (MIN-rulz) Natural elements that are not animals, plants, or other living things.

molecules (MAH-lih-kyoolz) The smallest bits of matter possible before they can be broken down into their basic parts.

nonfoliated (non-FOH-lee-ayt-ed) Having to do with metamorphic rocks that are smooth and do not have wavy lines of minerals.

plates (PLAYTS) The moving pieces of Earth's crust.

sediment (SEH-duh-ment) Mud, clay, or bits of rock carried by water.

sedimentary (seh-duh-MEN-teh-ree) Having to do with layers of stones, sand, or mud that have been pressed together to form rock.

temperature (TEM-pruh-cher) How hot or cold something is.

Index

Web Sites

Due to the changing nature of Internet links, PowerKids Press has developed an online list of Web sites related to the subject of this book. This site is updated regularly. Please use this link to access the list:

www.powerkidslinks.com/sres/metamorph/